LONGMAN LITERATURE GUIDELINES

I'M THE KING OF THE CASTLE
Susan Hill

by Theresa Sullivan

Series editors:
John Griffin
Theresa Sullivan

'Kingshaw is dominated by terror, and fear is the most appalling emotion to have to live with, day in day out, it is draining, depressing and demoralising. The future, once Kingshaw is told he is to go off to boarding school with Hooper, seems to hold out no hope at all; the fears will remain, the torments will be more varied and numerous, the prospect before Kingshaw's imagination is terrible indeed.'

Susan Hill, in the introduction to
I'm the King of the Castle (Longman Imprint Books)

Kingshaw and Hooper - victim and tormentor – these are the two main characters in a book which is of special relevance to students in your age group. Many of the themes that Susan Hill explores in *I'm the King of the Castle* – bullying, loneliness, fear – are problems that touch on your own closest concerns.

You will gain more benefit from the work presented here if you read *I'm the King of the Castle* first. The assignments ask you to explore Susan Hill's themes in greater depth by comparing passages from her novel with extracts from other novels, poems and plays which are on similar themes. You will be asked to act out extracts in order to test the dramatic nature of Susan Hill's dialogue; to take on the role of various characters in order to understand their different points of view; to assess the importance of the place and setting in a novelist's work and to relate your own experiences to those described in the novel. There is opportunity also to try your hand at different genres – newspaper reports, diary entries, police reports, plays and poems – in an attempt to widen your understanding of the important issues raised in *I'm the King of the Castle*.

Introduction

'Kingshaw is dominated by terror, and fear is the most appalling emotion to have to live with, day in day out, it is draining, depressing and demoralising. The future, once Kingshaw is told he is to go off to boarding school with Hooper, seems to hold out no hope at all; the fears will remain, the torments will be more varied and numerous, the prospect before Kingshaw's imagination is terrible indeed.'

Susan Hill, in the introduction to
I'm the King of the Castle (Longman Imprint Books)

Kingshaw and Hooper – victim and tormenter – these are the two main characters in a book which is of special relevance to students in your age group. Many of the themes that Susan Hill explores in *I'm the King of the Castle* – bullying, loneliness, fear – are problems that touch on your own closest concerns.

You will gain more benefit from the work presented here if you read *I'm the King of the Castle* first. The assignments ask you to explore Susan Hill's themes in greater depth by comparing passages from her novel with extracts from other novels, poems and plays which are on similar themes. You will be asked to act out extracts in order to test the dramatic nature of Susan Hill's dialogue; to take on the role of various characters in order to understand their different points of view; to assess the importance of the place and setting in a novelist's work; and to relate your own experiences to those described in the novel.

There is opportunity also to try your hand at different genres – newspaper reports, diary entries, police reports, plays and poems – in an attempt to widen your understanding of the important issues raised in *I'm the King of the Castle*.

Contents

I'm the King of the Castle: a children's game — 4
Why choose this title? — 4
Gaining the upper hand — 4
Hooper dares Kingshaw to pick up a moth — 5
Hooper is scared of the storm — 6
Kingshaw challenges Hooper to climb the castle — 7
Hooper locks Kingshaw in the shed — 7

Disputes over possessions and territory — 9
Territorial instincts — 10
This is my room — 11
We live here, we belong — 14

Bullies — 16
The Machine Gunners — 16
The dead crow — 17
The dare — 19
Being alive — 20
Advice for Kingshaw — 20
Does Kingshaw learn too late? — 21

Kingshaw at school — 22
First day at school — 22
This was all right — 23

Kingshaw's background — 24
Kes — 24
Compare Kingshaw's background to Billy's — 25

The parents — 27
Attitudes to parenthood — 28
The second marriage — 29
Parental responsibility — 29
The boy's attitude towards their parents — 30
Betrayal — 31

A sense of place and atmosphere — 32
Using birds to suggest the sinister — 34
Creating tension – the castle — 38

Kingshaw's suicide — 40
The future — 41
The shadow hanging over them — 41

Parallel themes in other works by Susan Hill — 42
'The Albatross' — 42
'The Elephant Man' — 45
'Friends of Miss Reece' — 46

I'm the King of the Castle: a children's game

You must have all played this game in your childhood. One child stands on something that gives him or her height – a wall or a table or a tree – and taunts the others who attempt to take his or her place with the rhyme:

'I'm the King of the Castle
Get down you dirty rascal!'

The rhyme must have a long history, going back to the times of barons and peasants. It tells us that throughout history men have desired to dominate others.

Why choose this title?

Why do you think Susan Hill has given her novel this title? Does it act as a clue to the book? The following assignments will help you to consider this.

▷ In groups of four, each take it in turns to be the 'master' of the group, giving orders to the 'slaves'. You might ask them to bring you a drink or tie your shoelace or bow down and worship you. When everyone has been master, discuss who you thought made the best master and why. Think about gesture, movement, posture and tone of voice. Is this person usually a leader?

▷ Try the exercise again, in two different ways. First, each person behave as a kind and generous master. Then each behave as a cruel and bullying master. This time, talk about the *differences* in behaviour, attitude, gesture and tone of voice.

Gaining the upper hand

▷ Use what you have learnt from the previous exercises. In pairs, one of you is Hooper and one Kingshaw. Prepare tableaux (still pictures, like freezing a frame in a film or video) of the following moments in the book.

Hooper dares Kingshaw to pick up a moth

Hooper came up behind him. 'Open one of the cases, then,' he said. 'I'll let you.' He held out a small key.

'No.'

'Why not?'

'I – I can see them all right, can't I?'

'Yes, but you can't touch them, can you. You've got to touch them.'

'No.'

'Why not? Scaredy-baby, scared of a moth!'

Kingshaw was silent. Hooper moved forward, inserted the key and pushed the heavy lid up.

'Pick one up.'

Kingshaw backed away. He could not have touched one for anything, and he did not want to watch Hooper do it.

'What's the matter, baby?'

'Nothing. I don't want to touch one, that's all.'

'They won't *hurt* you.'

'No.'

'They're dead, aren't they? They've been dead for years and years.'

'Yes.'

'What are you scared of? Are you scared of dead things?'

'No.'

Kingshaw went on moving backwards. He only wanted to get out of the room. If Hooper tried to grab him and force his hand down on to one of the moths, he would fight, he didn't care how much he fought.

'Come here and look, Kingshaw.'

'I don't want to.'

'Well *I* dare touch it, I'll pick one up and hold it. I dare do anything.'

'You'd better not.'

'Why?' Hopper was peering curiously into his face. 'Why?'

'You might damage it. If they're valuable you'll get into trouble, won't you?'

He imagined the furry body of the moth against the pads of Hooper's fingers. He was ashamed of being so afraid, and could not help it, he only wanted to get out, to stop having to see the terrible moths. Hooper watched him.

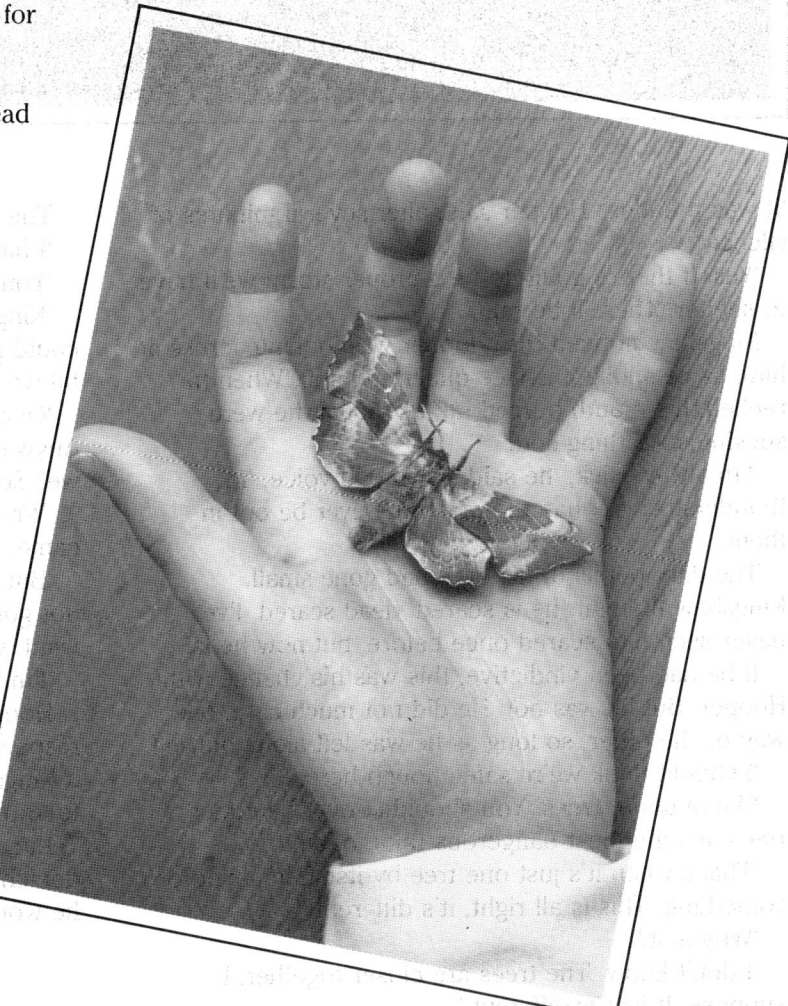

Hooper is scared of the storm

'It was thunder,' Hooper said, after several minutes of silence.

'Yes. If there's going to be a proper storm we'll have to shelter. There'll be rain.'

Kingshaw noticed that Hooper was looking across at him, as he spoke, his face queer and stiff. When he replied, his mouth pursed up, as though he were sucking something sour.

'I'm always sick,' he said, in an odd voice, 'in thunderstorms, I hate them. I can't ever be out in them.'

The dark pupils of his eyes had gone small. Kingshaw thought, he is scared, dead scared. I've never seen him scared once before, but now he is.

If he had been vindictive, this was his chance with Hooper. But he was not. He did not much care, one way or the other, so long as he was left alone himself.

'I should think we're safe enough here.'

'We're under trees. You shouldn't ever be under trees, it's the most dangerous thing of all.'

'That's when it's just one tree by itself, in a field or something. This is all right, it's different.'

'Why is it?'

'I don't know. The trees are closer together, I suppose. It just *is* different.'

The thunder rumbled again, not far away.

'I hate it, it makes me be sick.'

'You can be sick then, can't you? It won't matter.'

'Kingshaw, why can't we run for it? If we run we could get out, it mightn't start really properly storming till we get home.'

'Of course it would, we've come miles, haven't we? Anyway, for one, we don't know how to get out, do we? So how can we run home, stupid?'

'We could try, we can just go back the way we came.'

'But we don't know which way that is. Anyway, I'm not going back home, am I? You can do what you want, you can go.'

'I'm not being by myself in thunder.'

Hooper's voice had risen in panic. Whatever self-respect he might have had was gone, he did not care if Kingshaw saw that he was afraid – he *wanted* him to know, in fact, he wanted to be protected.

Kingshaw did not feel sorry for him at all. He was detached. But he wouldn't leave Hooper, he knew that he would have to take charge of things.

Kingshaw challenges Hooper to climb the castle

... Hooper shouted, 'I can come up if I want to.'

'Come on, then.'

'Those steps over there lead down into dungeons. *You* daren't go down to them.'

'Don't change the subject, Hooper. You daren't come up here and this is better than anything.'

Without warning, Kingshaw leaped over the gap between the stones of either wall and up on to the ledge. It was only just wide enough for his feet. He saw Hooper take in a sharp breath. His head was tilted back to watch, and the eyes and nostrils and mouth-hole were like black currants in his pale face. Kingshaw shouted, 'I bet you couldn't even walk along the first little bit of wall.'

Hooper locks Kingshaw in the shed

'I've got the key.'

'I don't care. They'll only come and look for me.'

'They wouldn't know where to start, they don't know about this place.'

'They'd find me in the end.'

'I'll tell them you've gone back to the wood.'

Kingshaw thought that there seemed to be no hope at all for him. He knelt down, and felt about carefully on the floor. But it was only concrete, cold and damp. He sat, hunching up his knees. Whatever happened, however long it lasted, he wouldn't ask Hooper to let him out, he wouldn't do anything at all, now, except sit here. The only thing that seemed to matter was that he should not give in.

'You're coming to school with me,' Hooper's voice went up and down in a sing-song.

Kingshaw was silent.

'You'll be in my dorm.'

'I might not.'

'Yes, you will, you'll be new. They'll put you in there because you've come with me and you live with us, they'll think it's what you want.'

'I don't care.'

'I'm Head of Dorm for next term.'

Kingshaw went cold. He knew that it was sure to be true, and that it would be the worst of all things that were coming. Hooper had power now, here. He would have power there, too, then.

'I can do what I like, and the others have got to do what I say. I can make anybody do anything to you.'

▷ Hooper has the upper hand in two of the moments and Kingshaw in the other two. Was there any difference in the way you portrayed each boy when he was master? Does this tell us anything about the boys?

Study these quotations from the novel:

He only thought, now, about the fact that he was alone with Hooper, and of what Hooper might do to him. Though perhaps he could do much less than in his own house. That was his territory, he was master. Here, they were somehow more equal. (Chapter 6)

But he was angry with himself for acknowledging Hooper's leadership. He tried to think of how he could get in front again himself. (Chapter 6)

Kingshaw heard, for the first time, a note of fear in Hooper's voice, and knew that he was leader, again, now. (Chapter 6)

Is the novel about the struggle between the two boys? What is it about them that means that Hooper will always win? Consider these quotations to help you:

If he had been vindictive, this was his chance with Hooper.

No, Kingshaw thought, no. Oh, Jesus, I am scared of him, I am.

In groups of four, each tackle a section of the book: at Warings (Chapters 1–4); in the wood (Chapters 5–9); Warings and the Castle (Chapters 10–14); Hooper returns home (Chapters 15–17).

Trace the struggles between the boys and present your results in a table like the one below, showing who wins each round.

What conclusions can you draw about the boys and their behaviour towards each other from your table?

▷ Choose one of the four sections of the book. Take on the role of either Hooper or Kingshaw, and write your account of the events, bringing out what you feel when you have gained the upper hand, and what you feel when the other boy has become the leader or the master.

Chapter 2	KINGSHAW	HOOPER
(1)		Hooper sends the note saying 'I DIDN'T WANT YOU TO COME HERE.'
(2) 'The photograph': 'Kingshaw knew that he had won, but he did not feel the winner.'		
(3)		The scrap – Kingshaw's bloody nose: 'I'll bash you again, just watch it.'

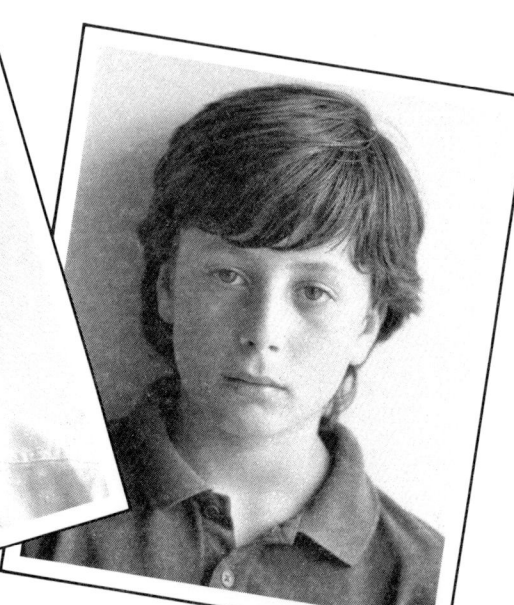

Disputes over possessions and territory

Read this piece written by someone who is frightened of dogs.

I've always been scared of dogs, right from when I was small and one nipped me on the arm. Whenever I see a dog in a street or on a farm, I immediately tense up and the dog senses it straightaway. They are supposed to be able to smell fear coming out of your body.

The dog begins to growl and crouch threateningly. As I get nearer, I stare straight ahead not daring to look at it but just keeping it in the corner of my eye. I walk stiffly trying to make myself as small as possible, and I clutch onto the arm of whoever's with me. The worst moment is when I've passed the dog. My back feels exposed and I don't know whether the creature won't snap at my ankles.

Then one day I made a huge discovery. I was walking through a farm with a friend who normally protects me in these circumstances, when a dog leapt out on us suddenly, barking so violently, that my friend shrieked and jumped in the air. The dog was going to take advantage of her fear, but when I saw this threat, I suddenly found my presence of mind and I snarled in a deep threatening voice: 'Get off with you!' and the dog slunk off quietly with his tail between his legs. I'd made the astonishing discovery that animals aren't any different from human beings!

Farm dogs are guarding their territory and will attack anyone who threatens that territory, though, of course, if they meet a person/animal who shows more aggression, they will back down. All dogs mark out their territory by urinating on the boundaries to warn off other dogs. They are, in this respect too, no more aggressive than human beings.

Territorial instincts

Kingshaw says of Warings in Chapter 6:

That was his [Hooper's] **territory, he was master. Here** [in the wood] **they were somehow more equal.**

How does this comment relate to what you have just read?

▷ Is defending one's territory a basic instinct that we share with animals? How much is this instinct a cause of war? Do you quarrel over possessions? Do you like to keep your bedroom private?

Look back at the tables you have drawn up. How many of the battles in the novel are over possessions?

▷ Chapters 1 and 2 are concerned to establish that Warings is Hooper's territory. Pick out two or three quotations designed to give this impression.

▷ How much of Kingshaw's trouble stems from the fact that he has no territory – no home he can call his own? Find two or three quotations to illustrate your answer.

Find two or three quotations to illustrate that Kingshaw feels happier in Hang Wood because he can make it his own territory. In what ways is he stronger than Hooper in the wood?

▷ 'This is all right. This is all right.' is repeated several times in the novel. When does Kingshaw say it? What is its significance?

What lesson might Kingshaw have learned from the person who was once frightened by dogs?

▷ Write about an occasion when you quarrelled with a brother or sister or friend over a possession. Compare your account with one of the incidents in which Kingshaw and Hooper quarrel over a possession.

The territorial instinct does not belong to children and animals alone. Read this extract from *The Caretaker* by Harold Pinter. Davies is a tramp who has been taken in by Aston. Aston's brother, Mick, however, comes back to find the tramp making himself at home, and he doesn't like it. Compare it with the passage on pages 14–15 where Kingshaw is given his room.

This is my room

Mick Did you sleep here last night?
Davies Yes.
Mick Sleep well?
Davies Yes!
Mick Did you have to get up in the night?
Davies No!
    Pause.
Mick What's your name?
Davies (*shifting, about to rise*). Now look here!
Mick. What?
Davies Jenkins!
Mick Jen . . kins.
    Davies makes a sudden move to rise. A violent bellow from Mick sends him back.
    (*A shout.*) Sleep here last night?
Davies Yes. . . .
Mick (*continuing at a great pace*). How'd you sleep?
Davies I slept –
Mick Sleep well?
Davies Now look –
Mick What bed?
Davies That –
Mick Not the other?
Davies No!
Mick Choosy.
    Pause.
    (*Quietly.*) Choosy.
    Pause.
    (*Again amiable.*) What sort of sleep did you have in that bed?
Davies (*banging the floor*). All right!
Mick You weren't uncomfortable?
Davies (*groaning*). All right!
    Mick stands, and moves to him.
Mick You a foreigner?
Davies No.
Mick Born and bred in the British Isles?
Davies I was!
Mick What did they teach you?
    Pause.
    How did you like my bed?
    Pause.

	That's my bed. You want to mind you don't catch a draught.
Davies	From the bed?
Mick	No, now, up your arse.

Davies stares warily at Mick, who turns. Davies scrambles to the clothes horse and seizes his trousers. Mick turns swiftly and grabs them. Davies lunges for them. Davies holds out a hand, warningly.

You intending to settle down here?

Davies Give me my trousers then.
Mick You settling down for a long stay?
Davies Give me my bloody trousers!
Mick Why, where you going?
Davies Give me and I'm going, I'm going to Sidcup!

Mick flicks the trousers in Davies face several times.
Davies retreats.
Pause.

Mick You know, you remind me of a bloke I bumped into once, just the other side of the Guildford by-pass –
Davies I was brought here!
Pause.
Mick Pardon?
Davies I was brought here! I was brought here!
Mick Brought here? Who brought you here?
Davies Man who lives here . . . he. . . .
Pause.
Mick Fibber.
Davies I was brought here, last night . . . met him in a caff . . . I was working . . . I got the bullet . . . I was working there . . . bloke saved me from a punch up, brought me here, brought me right here.
Pause.
Mick I'm afraid you're a born fibber, en't you? You're speaking to the owner. This is my room. You're standing in my house.
Davies It's his . . . he seen me all right . . . he. . . .
Mick (*pointing to Davies' bed*). That's my bed.
Davies What about that, then?
Mick That's my mother's bed.
Davies Well she wasn't in it last night!
Mick (*moving to him*) Now don't get perky, son, don't get perky. Keep your hands off my old mum.
Davies I ain't . . . I haven't. . . .
Mick Don't get out of your depth, friend, don't start taking liberties with my old mother, let's have a bit of respect.
Davies I got respect, you won't find anyone with more respect.
Mick Well, stop telling me all these fibs.
Davies Now listen to me, I never seen you before, have I?
Mick Never seen my mother before either, I suppose?
Pause.
I think I'm coming to the conclusion that you're an old rogue. You're nothing but an old scoundrel.
Davies Now wait –
Mick Listen, son. Listen, sonny. You stink.
Davies You ain't got no right to –

Mick You're stinking the place out. You're an old robber, there's no getting away from it. You're an old skate. You don't belong in a nice place like this. You're an old barbarian. Honest. You got no business wandering about in an unfurnished flat.

We live here, we belong

Hooper said, 'Why have you come here?' facing him across the room. Kingshaw flushed brick red. He stood his ground, not speaking. There was a small round table between them. His trunk and a suitcase stood on the floor. 'Why did you have to find somewhere new to live?'

Silence. Hooper thought, now I see why it is better to have a house like Warings. I see why my father goes about clutching the big bunch of keys. We live here, it is ours, we belong. Kingshaw has nowhere.

He walked round the table, towards the window. Kingshaw stepped back as he came.

'Scaredy!'

'No.'

'When my father dies,' Hooper said, 'this house will belong to me, I shall be master. It'll all be mine.'

'That's nothing. It's only an old house.'

Hooper remembered bitterly the land that his grandfather had been forced to sell off. He said quietly, 'Downstairs is something very valuable. Something you've never seen.'

'What then?'

Hooper smiled, looking away out of the window, choosing not to tell. And he was uncertain how impressive the moth collection might really be.

'My grandfather died in this room. Not very long ago, either. He lay and died in that bed. Now it's your bed.' This was not true.

Kingshaw went to the suitcase and squatted down.

'Where did you live before?'

'In a flat.'

'Where?'

'London.'

'Your *own* flat?'

'Yes – no. Well, it was in somebody's house.'

'You were only *tenants*, then.'

'Yes.'

'It wasn't really yours.'

'No.'

'Why didn't your father buy you a proper house?'

Kingshaw stood up. 'My father's dead.' He was angry, not hurt. He wanted to put his fists up to Hooper, and dared not.

Hooper raised his eyebrows. He had learned to do it from a master at school. It seemed an impressive way of looking.

'Well, my mother can't afford to buy us a house, can she? We can't help that.'

'Your father should have left you some money, then, shouldn't he? Didn't *he* have a house.'

'Yes, he did, it had to be sold.'

'Why?'

'I don't know.'

'To pay off all his debts.'

'No, no.'

'Do you remember your father?

'Oh, yes. Well – a bit. He was a pilot, once. He was in the Battle of Britain. I've got . . .' Kingshaw went down on his knees again, and began to search feverishly through the tartan suitcase. '. . . I've got a picture of him.'

'Is it a picture of him in the Battle?'

'No. But . . .'

'I don't believe you, anyway, you're a liar, the Battle of Britain was in the war.'

'Well, I know that, everybody knows that.'

'It was years ago, dozens of years. It was history. He couldn't have been in it.'

'He was, he was.'

'When did he die, then?'

'Here's the picture, look – that's my father.'

'*When did he die*, I said.' Hooper moved nearer, menacing.

'A few years ago. I was about five. Or six.'

'He would have been pretty old by then. How old was he?'

▷ In groups, discuss these questions. How are the situations similar? What similarities are there between Mick and Hooper? What differences? Does this tell us anything about Hooper? Do Kingshaw and Davies react in the same way? How are they different? What does this tell us about Kingshaw? How is this situation – and the behaviour of the people in it – parallelled in the animal kingdom?

Imagine that the situation was reversed and that the Kingshaws were offering Hooper a room. From your knowledge of the whole book, do you think Kingshaw would behave differently? Write an account – with dialogue – of Kingshaw's and Hooper's conversation as Hooper moves into the room.

▷ The book is about two boys and their relationship. Would it have been different if two girls had found themselves in the same situation? Do girls fight over territory and possessions in the same way?

In the first few pages of Chapter 2, Kingshaw arrives and settles in. In the light of your discussion, rewrite these pages as if Kingshaw and Hooper were two girls. Choose names for them.

Bullies

Chas McGill in *The Machine Gunners* by Robert Westall, is pursued by Boddser Brown, the school bully. Boddser has chased Chas all through the town and has caught up with him at the swamps near the river. Compare the following passage in the *The Machine Gunners* in which Boddser bullies Chas, with the passage from *I'm the King of the Castle* on pages 17–18 in which Hooper bullies Kingshaw by putting the dead crow on his bed.

The Machine Gunners

Chas looked round desperately, but there was no way out except the path Boddser Brown stood astride. Nor was there anything to hit Boddser with. He wrenched at a rib of the old boat, but his hand just slipped on the oozing wood. Next minute he was lying face-down on the wet grass with one arm twisted behind his back, and Boddser's knee on his neck. He twisted his head, for black water was getting into his nostrils and mouth.

'Geroff, you swine,' he snarled; it was a gesture without hope.

'Poor old Chassy McGill,' crooned Boddser, with evil sentimentality. 'Where's your brains now, Chas?' He twisted Chas's arm up tighter. 'Why don't you shout for help? Go on, shout.'

Chas shouted. It couldn't do any harm.

'Louder!' Boddser twisted Chas's arm tighter. 'Louder!' He gave another twist. 'Louder!'

Nobody came.

'Right, to business,' said Boddser briskly, moving his knee from Chas's neck to the small of his back. 'Where's that machine-gun?'

'Sod off,' gasped Chas. He gave a vigorous squirm that half threw Boddser off, and crawled for dear life. But it only made things worse. He was now hanging face down over a little black stream. And he knew what was coming next.

'Thank you, McGill,' said Boddser. 'That's saved me a lot of trouble.' Chas took a deep breath and closed his mouth as his head was thrust under water. He was under a long time, while his chest swelled and swelled until it felt it would burst. Then his head was released. He breathed out. He felt Boddser's hand coming down to push him under again before he could breath in. He moved his head quickly and Boddser's hand slipped. Chas snatched a breath before he went under again. He felt strangely calm.

After half-an-hour, Boddser began to get worried. Things were not turning out as usual. Usually, by this time, kids were blubbing, begging for mercy, willing to do anything; which made Boddser feel hot and good and squelchy inside, and then he'd let the kids go.

But McGill wasn't like that. He just went on spitting out swear-words, whenever he had the breath. And once, when Boddser's hand had slipped, McGill had bitten his wrist hard and savage, like a dog. Boddser stared fascinated at the horse-shoe of teethmarks in his own precious flesh. They hurt; they seeped blood into the muddy wetness of his arm. Boddser started to fret. The dirty water might turn the wound septic.

And now McGill lay silent, motionless, breathing in a funny sort of way. Had he fainted, or had a fit? He had acted so queerly. But Boddser gave his arm a twist.

'Want some more, McGill?' There was no response. Boddser got to his feet, suddenly shaking, terrified. What had he done?

Next minute, McGill was up and gone, running now like a small muddy rat. Boddser roared with rage and pursued. Fooled again!

McGill crossed the first plank-bridge and seemed to fall. 'Got you!' roared Boddser and made to cross the plank. Chas twisted round, caught the end of the plank and threw it into the water. Boddser, unable to stop, went into the stream up to his waist. The coldness of the water made him gasp. By the time he'd scrambled out, McGill had crossed the next plank and thrown that in the water too.

The dead crow

What he saw first was not the clock. There was a thin beam of moonlight coming into the room, and a shape upon his bed, about half way down. He could not at all make out what it was. He listened. Somebody had been in his room, but there was no sound, now, from outside the door.

He thought, make me put the light on, I mustn't be too scared to put the light on, I've got to see. But he dared not reach out his hand, he lay stiff, his eyes wide open. Nothing moved. He did not move.

But he had to see, had to know. Make me, make me put on the light . . .

He reached out his left hand swiftly, and found the switch and pressed it before he could stop himself. He looked.

He knew at once that the crow was not real, that it was stuffed and dead. Somehow, that only made it so much worse. Its claws were gripping the sheet. It was very big.

Kingshaw lay stiff, and did not scream, did not make any sound at all. He was dry and faint with fear of the thing, though his brain still worked, he knew who had brought it, he knew that Hooper was still waiting out in the corridor, must have seen the light go on. Hooper wanted him to be frightened, to scream and cry and shout for his mother. He would not do that. There was nothing, nothing at all, that he could do to help himself. He wanted to lift up his leg quickly, and topple the terrible bird on to the floor, out of sight, not to have it there, pressing down on his thigh. But if he moved at all, it might fall all the wrong way – forwards, nearer to him. He would not be able to touch it with his hand.

He must put out the light. Hooper was still waiting, listening. He managed it, eventually, but he dared not draw his hand back into the bed. He lay with his eyes squeezed shut, and a burning pain in his bladder. He was afraid of wetting the bed. He wished to be dead, he wished Hooper dead. But there was nothing, nothing he could do. In the end, towards morning, he half-slept.

When he woke again, it was just after six o'clock. The crow looked even less real, now, but much larger. He lay and waited for the beak to open so that he would see the scarlet inside of its mouth, for it to rise up and swoop down at him, making for his eyes. He thought, it's stupid, it's stupid, it's only a stupid, rotten bird. He took one deep breath, and then closed his eyes and rolled over, out of bed on to the floor. Then, ran. He sat for a long time on the lavatory. The house was quite silent.

He wondered what he could do with the thing, how he could possibly get rid of it. Now it was daylight, he would be even more afraid of touching it with his bare hands, but he wouldn't tell anyone about its presence in his room. It would have to stay there, then, lie on the floor beside his bed, night after night, until Mrs Boland came to clean and took it away.

But when he got back, the crow had gone.

▷ In groups, use the passages to help you to understand the nature of Hooper's bullying and Kingshaw's reactions. What have Kingshaw and Chas got in common? How are they different? How does Hooper's bullying differ from Boddser's? What does their chosen method of bullying tell us about them as people? Which kind of bullying do you find more frightening or repulsive? How would Kingshaw react if he were in Chas' place? How do you know?

▷ Kingshaw has been bullied by someone like Boddser Brown. His name was Crawford and you will find the account near the beginning of Chapter 15. Imagine that a sympathetic teacher is questioning Kingshaw about the incident and how it happened. Write your interview between the teacher and the boy in the form of a play.

▷ Write about a time when you were bullied or witnessed someone being bullied.

Read Judith Nicholl's poem 'The dare'. Consider the reasons why she is frightened of the dare and then why she accepts it.

The dare

*Go on, I dare you,
come on down!*

Was it me they called?
Pretend you haven't heard,
a voice commanded in my mind.
Walk past, walk fast
and don't look down,
don't look behind.

Come on, it's easy!

The banks were steep,
the water low
and flanked with oozing brown.
Easy? Walk fast
but don't look down.
Walk straight, walk on,
even risk their jeers
and run. . .

Never go near those dykes,
my mother said.
No need to tell me.
I'd seen stones sucked in
and covered without trace,
gulls slide to bobbing safety,
grasses drown as water rose.
No need to tell me
to avoid the place.

*She ca-a-a-n't, she ca-a-a-n't!
Cowardy, cowardy custard!*

There's no such word as 'can't',
my father said.
I slowed my pace.
The voices stopped,
waited as I wavered, grasping breath.
My mother's wrath? My father's scorn?
A watery death?

I hesitated then turned back,
forced myself to see the mud below.
After all, it was a dare. . .
There was no choice;
I had to go.

Judith Nicholl

▷ In groups, collect together all the dares you can find in the book. How many are Hooper's? How many are Kingshaw's? Does either boy ever dare himself? How does Fielding respond to a dare?

When Hooper is stuck on the wall of the castle he says 'It's your fault, you dared me', and Kingshaw replies 'I never did'. Is this true?

▷ Compare Kingshaw's reactions to a dare with those in the poem. Are they similar or different? How? Compare Kingshaw's reactions with Fielding's.

It is through Kingshaw's responses to dares that Hooper knows he can bully and intimidate him. How does Hooper know?

What does this tell us about the three boys?

▷ Mrs Kingshaw says, 'It isn't always the people who have no fears at all, who are the bravest, you know', when Kingshaw has accused Hooper of acting like a baby in the thunderstorm. What does she mean? Do you agree with her? Is Kingshaw brave because he has to cope with such strong fears?

D.H. Lawrence in his poem 'Being alive' gives advice on how to be fully alive. Not all of the advice would be relevant to, or have any meaning for, a little boy like Kingshaw – he isn't old enough to feel that he needs to 'get money', for instance.

Being alive

The only reason for living is being fully alive;
and you can't be fully alive if you are crushed by secret
   fear,
and bullied with the threat: Get money, or eat dirt! –
and forced to do a thousand mean things meaner than
   your nature,
and forced to clutch on to possessions in the hope they'll
   make you feel safe,
and forced to watch everyone that comes near you, lest
   they've come to do you down.

Without a bit of common trust in one another, we can't
   live.
In the end, we go insane.
It is the penalty of fear and meanness, being meaner
   than our natures are.

To be alive, you've got to feel a generous flow,
and under a competitive system that is impossible,
   really.
The world is waiting for a new great movement of
   generosity,
or for a great wave of death.
We must change the system, and make living free to all
   men,
or we must see men die, and then die ourselves.

                                        D.H. Lawrence

Advice for Kingshaw

▷ In groups, discuss which particular pieces of advice in the poem are relevant to Kingshaw? Does anybody in the novel give him any of this advice? Why is he incapable of accepting the advice and putting it into practice?

Here is Susan Hill's own comment on her character:

> '.... some of the time one does want to shake him, tell him to pull himself together, stop being such a weed, face his terrors, stand his ground ....'

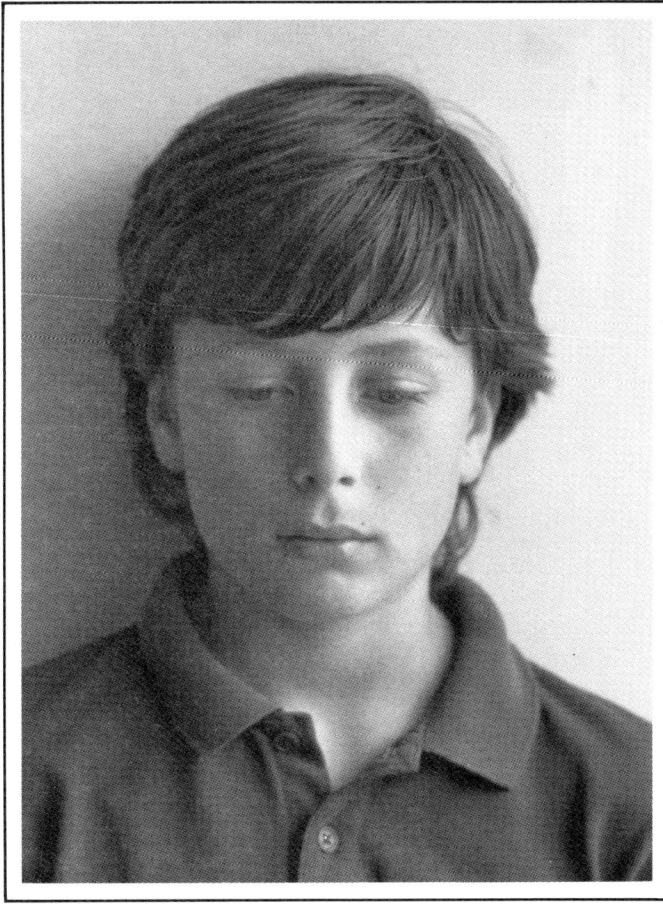

▷ Does this reflect your own feelings about Kingshaw?

▷ Write your own poem of advice to Kingshaw. Imitate D.H. Lawrence's style which gives the appearance of somebody talking, making a series of strong statements, each of which forms a line in the poem.

Does Kingshaw learn too late?

Read this extract from the novel and in groups decide what it is that Kingshaw learns here. Has he learnt it too late? Does being easy and not caring as Fielding is, make you safe against the attacks of other people? Think of people you know and how they respond to being dared or being bullied.

Inside the Red Room, Fielding said, 'Hey – it's butterflies! Great!'

'Moths,' Hooper said, 'Moths are different. They're better than butterflies.'

Fielding was peering down eagerly into the first case. 'I can see them properly, now. I can see all the hairs on their bodies.'

Kingshaw stiffened.

'My grandfather collected these. He was world-famous, he wrote books and things about them. They're worth thousands of pounds.'

'Liar.'

Hooper turned on Kingshaw. 'You just stuff it, scaredy. You don't know anything.'

At once, Fielding glanced round, anxiously. Kingshaw refused to meet his eye. Hooper was moving over to the display cases, looking closely at Fielding's face again. 'Dare you *touch* one?'

Fielding looked puzzled. 'Yes. They're only dead things. They can't hurt you.'

'Go on then.'

'It's locked, though.'

'No, it isn't, you can lift the lid up.'

'Wouldn't they get damaged? We might get into trouble.'

'*I* dare touch one. I lifted one out, once.'

'Oh.'

Fielding had walked to the next case. From the doorway, watching them, Kingshaw thought, Hooper believes him, he isn't going to make him open the case and put his hand on one, he isn't going to make him prove it, he just believes him. That's the way Fielding is, that's the way you should be.

It had been different with him. Hooper had known, from the very first moment he had looked into Kingshaw's face, that it would all be easy, that he would always be able to make him afraid. Why, thought Kingshaw, *why*? His eyes suddenly pricked with tears, at the unfairness of it. WHY?

▷ Imagine that you are Fielding. Write your account of your first meeting with Kingshaw, bringing out your impressions of him.

Kingshaw at school

Read this poem about the feelings of a small child on his first day at school and compare it with what we learn of Kingshaw's first weeks at school (page 23).

First day at school

A millionbillionwillion miles from home
Waiting for the bell to go. (To go where?)
Why are they all so big, other children?
So noisy? So much at home they
must have been born in uniform
Lived all their lives in playgrounds
Spent the years inventing games
that don't let me in. Games
that are rough, that swallow you up.

And the railings.
All around, the railings.
Are they to keep out wolves and monsters?
Things that carry off and eat children?
Things you don't take sweets from?
Perhaps they're to stop us getting out
Running away from the lessins. Lessin.
What does a lessin look like?
Sounds small and slimy.
They keep them in glassrooms.
Whole rooms made out of glass. Imagine.

I wish I could remember my name

Mummy said it would come in useful.
Like wellies. When there's puddles.
Yellowwellies. I wish she was here.
I think my name is sewn on somewhere
Perhaps the teacher will read it for me.
Tea-cher. The one who makes the tea.

                        Roger McGough

This was all right

He thought about school. There, he belonged, they knew him, he had become the person they had all decided that he would be. It was safe. The first day he had arrived, when the car had stopped in front of Main Block, he had known it would be all right, it was what he wanted. Lots of the others had been crying, and white in the face, their mothers held their hands. He had not cried. He had wanted to go inside and see everything, to look at the faces of those who were already there, touch the walls and the doors and the cover of his bed, smell the particular smells. He had been tense with excitement, feeling his feet crunch on the gravel, he had wanted to say to his mother, go away, go away, so that it could all begin.

'How brave!' somebody else's mother had said.

'Oh, but they do not always show everything, he is bottling it up. He is only seven, and that is no age, no age at all.'

Mrs Helena Kingshaw said, 'Charles is a very sensible little boy. Though – oh, yes, I wonder so often if we are doing the right thing, if he is not still too young . . .'

But they had, they had, Kingshaw thought, fingering the embossed badge on his new blazer. This was all right, it was what he wanted. Though it was different, he could not have imagined what it would be like.

The third week of term, he had been ill. He was in a special room and everybody had come to see him whenever they liked, and he had books and biscuits and any drink that he asked for. The sun had shone through the window on to his bed. He thought this is all right, this is the place to be. When he got up, he could go into the Headmaster's house and watch television and eat fruit.

▷ What is the difference in tone between the two accounts? Does this tell us anything about Kingshaw? What is the difference in attitude between the two boys. Why can the boy in the poem joke and Kingshaw can't? Why did Kingshaw particularly value school?

▷ Imagine that you are Kingshaw. Write a poem about your first day at school. Like Roger McGough's poem, it need not rhyme.

Kingshaw's background

Billy Caspar, like Kingshaw, has no father. But, although Kingshaw feels underprivileged compared with Hooper and the boys at school, his background is very different from Billy's. Read this extract from A Kestrel for a Knave by Barry Hines.

Kes

The estate was teeming with children: tots hand in hand with their mothers, tots on their own, and with other tots, groups of tots and Primary School children; Secondary School children, on their own, in pairs and in threes, in gangs and on bikes. Walking silently, walking on walls, walking and talking, quietly, loudly, laughing; running, chasing, playing, swearing, smoking, ringing bells and calling names: all on their way to school.

When Billy arrived home, the curtains were still drawn in all the front windows, but the light was on in the living-room. As he crossed the front garden, a man appeared from round the side of the house and walked up the path to the gate. Billy watched him walk away down the avenue, then ran round to the back door and into the kitchen.

'Is that you, Reg?'

Billy banged the door and walked through into the living-room. His mother was standing in her underslip, a lipstick poised at her mouth, watching the doorway through the mirror. When she saw Billy, she started to apply the lipstick.

'O, it's you, Billy. Haven't you gone to school yet?'

'Who's that bloke?'

His mother pressed her lips together and stood the capsule, like a bullet, on the mantelpiece.

'That's Reg. You know Reg, don't you?

She took a cigarette packet from the mantelpiece and shook it.

'Hell! I forgot to ask him for one.'

She dropped the packet into the hearth and turned to Billy.

'You haven't got a fag on you, have you, love?'

Billy moved across to the table and placed both hands round the teapot. His mother pulled her skirt on and tried to zip it on the hip. The zip would only close half-way, so she secured the waistband with a safety pin. The zip slipped as soon as she moved, and the slit expanded to the shape of a rugby ball. Billy shoved a finger down the spout of the teapot.

'Is that him you come home wi' last night?'

'There's some tea mashed if you want a cup, but I don't know if t'milk's come or not.'

'Was it?'

'Oh, stop pestering me! I'm late enough as it is.'

She crumpled her sweater into a tyre and eased her head through the hole, trying to prevent her hair from touching the sides.

'Do me a favour, love, and run up to t'shop for some fags.'

'They'll not be open yet.'
'You can go to t'back door. Mr Hardy'll not mind.'
'I can't, I'll be late.'
'Go on, love, and bring a few things back wi' you; a loaf and some butter, and a few eggs, summat like that.'
'Go your sen.'
'I've not time. Just tell him to put it in t'book and I'll pay him at t'week-end.'
'He says you can't have owt else 'til you've paid up.'
'He always says that. I'll give you a tanner if you go.'
'I don't want a tanner. I'm off now.'
He moved towards the door, but his mother stepped across and blocked his way.
'Billy, get up to that shop and do as you're telled.'
He shook his head. His mother stepped forward, but he backed off, keeping the same distance between them. Although she was too far away, she still swiped at him, and although he saw her hand coming, and going, well clear of his face, he still flicked his head back instinctively.
'I'm not going.'
He moved behind the table.
'Aren't you? We'll see about that.'
They faced each other across the table, their fingers spread on the cloth, like two pianists ready to begin.
'An' there's a bet of our Jud's to take, an' all. You'd better not forget that.'
'I'm not taking it.'
'You'd better, lad.'
'I'm fed up o'taking 'em. He can take it his sen.'
'How can he, you dozy bugger, if he don't get home in time?'
'I don't care, I'm not taking it.'
'Please yourself then. . . .'

Compare Kingshaw's background to Billy's

What details do you learn from the extract about Billy's background and way of life. Find details from Kingshaw's life which contrast with this. Compare the way the characters speak in *I'm the King of the Castle* with the way Billy and his mother speak. How do you think Kingshaw would survive in an environment like Billy's? Compare Billy's mother with Mrs Kingshaw. What similarities and differences are there in their attitude to their sons? Does Kingshaw's background make it harder or easier for him?

▷ Billy too likes wandering in the woods outside his home town, trying to escape from his family. Imagine that it were possible for him to meet Kingshaw in the countryside, as Kingshaw meets Fielding. Write an account of their meeting. How would they get on? What would they talk about? Would they have to explain the way that they lived?

The parents

'They [Mrs Kingshaw and Mr Hooper] are rather two-dimensional characters, and deliberately so; they are formalised even in speech-style (whereas the boys talk, I hope, as eleven year-old boys do talk). We are distanced from the adults, and do not go far inside their minds and emotions.'

Susan Hill

▷ Use the following extract to decide what Susan Hill means by 'they are formalised even in speech-style'.

'Now I am going back to the hospital, dear, in just a few minutes. But you will be quite all right with Mrs Boland.'

'Yes.'

Kingshaw discarded a piece of sky, and sorted about for another. All the pieces looked the same.

'Mr Hooper has gone to London.'

'Yes.'

'And he is not going to be back until tomorrow, so you will be very good by yourself, won't you?'

'Yes.'

He fidgeted about in the jigsaw box, rattling the pieces, willing her to go away.

'Of course I must go and see poor Edmund.'

'All right.'

'Perhaps tomorrow you might be able to come to the hospital with me – yes, now that *is* a good idea! I shall remember to ask Sister.'

'No,' he said hastily. 'I don't want to. Thank you.'

'Why ever not?'

'No.'

'It would cheer him up, I know, to have his friend visit him.'

'Look, I don't *want* to go, that's all.'

He tried to force a wrong piece into the jigsaw, and bent one of the cardboard prongs.

'Well . . . we'll see . . .'

'I'm not going.'

'Let's not argue about it now, Charles, please. And it *is* such a lovely day, I cannot think why you must sit in here doing a puzzle. That is a thing for a *wet* day, isn't it?'

He shrugged.

'I think you had far better go out and enjoy the fresh air and lovely sunshine, while you can. It will be cold again, before we know where we are.'

Kingshaw turned his attention from the sky of the puzzle, to the river part, on the bottom. But that looked nearly as hard. It was the only jigsaw in the house.

'Have you anything you want me to tell Edmund, dear?'

'No.'

'But I think it would be so nice, if you could just think up some little message, you know.'

▷ Susan Hill says that she has deliberately made the parents 'two-dimensional' – that is, we do not go very far into their feelings and motives. Why do you think she has done this? Does this stop us from feeling too much sympathy for them? Does it increase the concentration on the conflict between the two boys?

Attitudes to parenthood

The parents continually worry about whether they are bringing up their boys correctly as these extracts show.

Perhaps I should strike him, Joseph Hooper thought, for speaking to me in that way, perhaps it is very foolish to let him get the upper hand, to allow such insolence. I do not like his supercilious expression. I should assert myself. But he knew that he would not. He deliberated too long, and then it could not be done. I have tried to avoid my own father's mistakes, he said, but I have only succeeded in replacing them with so many of my own.

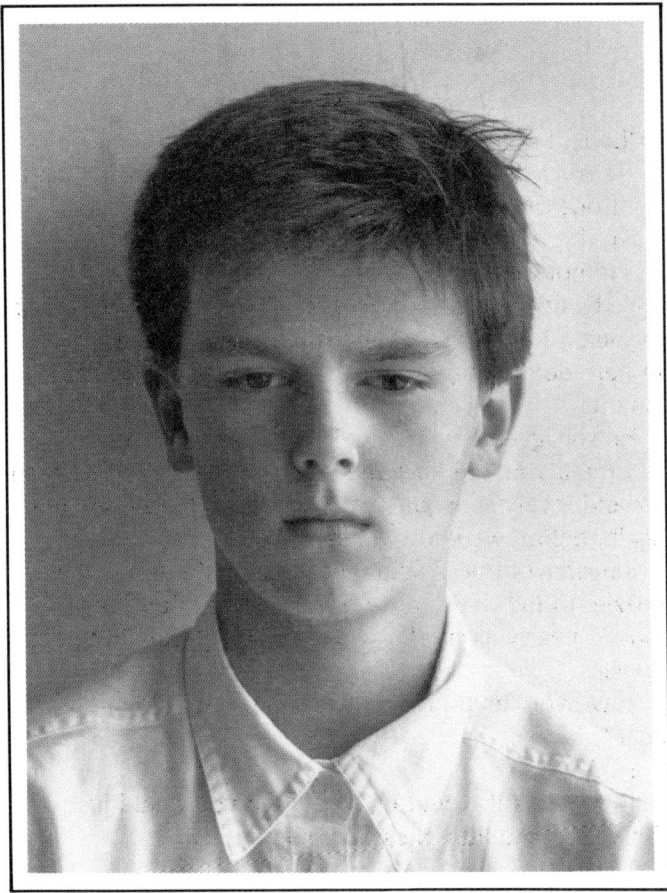

Mr Hooper coughed, turned his face away, and shifted a little in his seat. There is no telling, he thought, perhaps he does remember something of his mother, after all. We cannot fathom the minds of young children. He was discomforted by his own lack of insight. He tried to find some clue, in his son's facial expression, as to what might be going on in his mind, but there was only a blank. He could recall nothing of himself at the same age except that he had loathed his own father.

But I came through, he said to himself now, I daresay that I am normal enough, that there is nothing so much wrong with me, in spite of it all. I shall not allow myself to feel guilty about it. Edmund will be like any other healthy boy. I am not to blame.

She felt a little ashamed of not wanting to take Charles with her. He said, 'I wouldn't want to go, anyway. I'd rather stay here.' She would not let herself believe it, for she worried a good deal about her own capacity for motherhood, about whether she said the right things and looked sufficiently at ease, in his presence.

Now, she said, I must think of myself a little more, and opened the door of her wardrobe, to begin the choosing of clothes to wear.

▷ What do you learn from these extracts about the relationship Mrs Kingshaw and Mr Hooper have with their sons? Do they understand them? Or do they have problems of their own which make them unable to understand? Would it have made any difference to the events of the novel, if they had been different? What does Hooper think of his father? What does Kingshaw think of his mother?

▷ Find other extracts in which the parents think and talk about how they bring up their children. Imagine that each of them is telling a friend about their attitudes towards parenting and how they have dealt with events up to the boys' return from Hang Wood (Chapter 10). Write each of their conversations.

Attitudes to parenthood

The second marriage

As the boys struggle more fiercely, the parents become closer, as these extracts show.

Kingshaw stopped. His mother had said, 'You should be very, very polite to Mr Hooper. He has been so very kind to us already. He is anxious to take an interest in you, Charles, already he has been talking to me about your schooling and your future.' Her eyes had been very bright, and the bracelets went sliding up and down her arm. Do not spoil everything for me, she wanted to say, do not take away my chance. Kingshaw did not like this new eagerness and hopefulness about her, now that she was at Warings.
    She had changed a good deal.

They were gratified with one another, and with this new arrangement of their lives, and so it was easy to say, 'How well the boys have settled down together! How nice to see them enjoying themselves! How good it is for them not to be alone!' For they talked at length about their children, knowing nothing of the truth.
    Mrs Helena Kingshaw threw herself eagerly into the planning of the Sunday morning cocktail party, to which so many important people were invited. She thought, my life is changing, everything is turning out for the best. Oh, how right I was to come here!

'I have built a good fire in the sitting room,' said Mr Joseph Hooper, smoothing back his hair, hovering in the doorway of the kitchen. 'Perhaps you would care to come and sit in there, keep me company and so forth. Just as a change.'
    Mrs Helena Kingshaw blushed, and made a little gesture of surprise and pleasure.

▷ What is each parent's motive in becoming closer? Are we intended to sympathise with their growing relationship? Give your reasons. Does their desire for each other blind them to their sons' needs? Or do they pretend to ignore what they don't want to realise?

▷ Imagine that you are Mrs Kingshaw. Write a letter to a friend telling her that you are about to remarry. Describe Mr Hooper and his son and your feelings towards them, and say how you think your son is taking the situation.

Parental responsibility

Mr Hooper and Mrs Kingshaw do not find parenthood easy; their sons puzzle them. But it could be argued that their growing interest in each other made them negligent during the episode at Leydell Castle.

▷ Work in groups of three. Imagine that one of you is a local reporter looking for a good story who hears about Hooper's fall. The other two take on the roles of Mrs Kingshaw and Hooper. The reporter must cross-examine them closely about what they were doing at the time, how responsible or guilty they feel about what happened, and what compensation they will make in future.

Write up your interview in the form of a play.

▷ Discuss what you think Susan Hill means by the following remark about her characters.

> 'Both Mrs Kingshaw and Mr Hooper are to some extent still at odds with the normal, adult world.'
>
> Susan Hill

The boys' attitude towards their parents

Read this extract in which Hooper turns Kingshaw against his mother.

'Your mother goes upstairs to see you, I know, because I hear her. She has to kiss you good-night like a little baby.'

'Boil your head. She doesn't always come.'

'Yes, she does, then. Kiss, kiss, kiss. Oh, there, my little darling, dear little baby-boy, Mummy loves her little babyboy, Mummy goes cuddle, cuddle, cuddle, every night, little diddums baby – that's what.'

'Just because you haven't got a mother at all.'

But Hooper was unmoved. 'I wouldn't want one.'

'That's a stupid thing to say.'

'Fathers are better. Anybody who hasn't got a father is useless.'

Kingshaw stood up and went nearer to the fire. Hooper looked at him. Kingshaw was holding a long, thick stick in his right hand. For a moment, neither of them moved. He saw Hooper's eyes widen.

'You'd better not try and hit me.'

Kingshaw looked down at him scornfully, and then threw the stick on to the fire. The flames leaped up, throwing a shadow behind him, on to the grass.

'If you don't want to catch fire, you'd better move back out of the way.'

Hooper only went on, staring into the blaze. He said casually, 'Has your mother gone after a lot of people?'

'What do you mean?'

'I mean like she's gone after my father.'

Kingshaw felt the blood coming up into his face. He seemed to be going hotter and hotter, right inside himself. He thought, I was stupid, I could have bashed him with that stick, bashed and bashed his head in.

Now, Hooper was leaning on his elbow, looking up, his face prideful, in the flickering light from the bonfire. Gloating.

'That's why you came here. You didn't think it was for anything else, did you? She wants to be married to my father. He's rich.'

'Liar, liar, liar. Your father isn't anything, she doesn't even like your father. She hates him.'

Hooper smiled. 'There are things I see that you don't.'

'What? What things?'

'Never mind. But you've got to believe me.'

'Your father's nothing.'

'Look, it's all right, Kingshaw, it's only what ladies do. If she hasn't got a husband, she's got to find one.'

'Why has she?'

'Well, because he'd give her money and a house and things, that's what always happens.'

Kingshaw walked slowly away from the fire. He couldn't go on answering back, having a stupid argument. Hooper always wanted to keep up for hours. But it was all true, he could see that.

He hated his mother more than anybody, more even than Hooper, now. He had a terrible twisted-up feeling in his belly, because of it. Now, Hooper knew. 'There are things I see that you don't.'

There wasn't anything he could do. Except get away. It was his father's fault, really, because his dying had been the start of it all, the not having enough money, and living in other people's houses. Even at school, he couldn't forget it. People had found out that he was a G.B.B. – a Governor's Bequest Boy, which meant he didn't pay fees any more. His mother made things worse. She came on speech day and sports day, all got up with earrings and awful, slippery-looking dresses, and started putting on lipstick where everybody could see. Brace had said, 'Kingshaw's mother's an old tart.'

▷ How has Hooper exploited what Kingshaw has always feared about his mother? Why is it a good taunt of Hooper's to tease Kingshaw about his mother's kissing him?

Find other extracts from the book in which the boys talk about or think about their parents.

Betrayal

In Chapter 10 Hooper breaks any trust the parents might have in Kingshaw and so puts him in a very difficult position.

▷ How does Hooper trap Kingshaw? How does this make it difficult for Mr Hooper and Mrs Kingshaw to believe him. How does this begin a new attitude in Mrs Kingshaw towards Hooper? What leads Kingshaw to the belief that 'people are no good, then, people can never help me'?

Analyse Kingshaw's behaviour and consider how it seems from the outside. Could Kingshaw have helped himself?

A sense of place and atmosphere

'... settings are always very, very important to me, every bit as much as characters or themes.'

Susan Hill

▷ Susan Hill takes care to give us a detailed picture of Warings, particularly of the rooms which are relevant to the boys. Imagine that you are Kingshaw writing a letter to Devereux in which you describe what Warings is like and its setting. Certain rooms, like the Red Room and the room at the top of the house, you will be able to describe in more detail. You will find what you need in the first four chapters of the book.

▷ The room at the top of the house is Kingshaw's special private place and is described in some detail. Draw a ground plan of the room, placing all the objects in it. You will find the information you need at the beginning of Chapter 4.

▷ Draw a map of the journey along the stream in the wood, and mark it with the events that happen along it, the objects the boys find, and any geographical details. Start from where the boys can hear the stream below them and decide to follow it. The first thing they find is the dead rabbit. You will find the information you need in Chapters 7 and 8.

▷ Draw a picture of Hang Wood. Frame it with quotations from the novel which describe the wood.

▷ Draw a picture of the castle with the figures of the two boys on it. Frame it with quotations from Kingshaw and Hooper.

Using birds to suggest the sinister

One of the many terrifying experiences Kingshaw undergoes is the attack by the crow. Birds have often been used in literature to suggest the sinister. Hitchcock produced a horror film from a story by Daphne du Maurier called 'The Birds'. In this extract from *The Dark is Rising*, the writer, Susan Cooper, is using an attack by rooks to suggest that something mysterious and supernatural is about to happen. Compare it with the extract in which Kingshaw is attacked by a crow (pages 36–37).

The noise from the rookery was louder, even though the daylight was beginning to die. They could see the dark birds thronging over the treetops, more agitated than before, flapping and turning to and fro. And Will had been right; there was a stranger in the lane, standing beside the churchyard.

He was a shambling, tattered figure, more like a bundle of old clothes than a man, and at the sight of him the boys slowed their pace and drew instinctively closer to the cart and to one another. He turned his shaggy head to look at them.

Then suddenly, in a dreadful blur of unreality, a hoarse, shrieking flurry was rushing dark down out of the sky, and two huge rooks swooped at the man. He staggered back, shouting, his hands thrust up to protect his face, and the birds flapped their great wings in a black vicious whirl and were gone, swooping up past the boys and into the sky.

Will and James stood frozen, staring, pressed against the bales of hay.

The stranger cowered back against the gate.

'Kaaaaaaak . . . kaaaaaak . . .' came the head-splitting racket from the frenzied flock over the wood, and then three more whirling black shapes were swooping after the first two, diving wildly at the man and then away.

This time he screamed in terror and stumbling out into the road, his arms still wrapped in defence round his head, his face down; and he ran. The boys heard the frightened gasps for breath as he dashed headlong past them, and up the road past the gates of Dawsons' Farm and on towards the village. They saw bushy, greasy grey hair below a dirty old cap; a torn brown overcoat tied with string, and some other garment flapping beneath it; old boots, one with a loose sole that made him kick his leg oddly sideways, half-hopping, as he ran. But they did not see his face.

The high whirling above their heads was dwindling into loops of slow flight, and the rooks began to settle one by one into the trees. They were still talking loudly to one another in a long cawing jumble, but the madness and the violence were not in it now. Dazed, moving his head for the first time, Will felt his cheek brush against something, and putting his hand to his shoulder, he found a long black feather there. He pushed it into his jacket pocket, moving slowly, like someone half-awake.

Together they pushed the loaded cart down the road to the house, and the cawing behind them died to an ominous murmur, like the swollen Thames in spring.

James said at last, 'Rooks don't do that sort of thing. They don't attack people. And they don't come down low when there's not much space. They just don't.'

When he first saw the crow, he took no notice. There had been several crows. This one glided down into the corn on its enormous, ragged black wings. He began to be aware of it when it rose up suddenly, circled overhead, and then dived, to land not very far away from him. Kingshaw could see the feathers on its head, shining black in between the butter-coloured cornstalks. Then it rose, and circled, and came down again, this time not quite landing, but flapping about his head, beating its wings and making a sound like flat leather pieces being slapped together. It was the largest crow he had ever seen. As it came down for the third time, he looked up and noticed its beak, opening in a screech. The inside of its mouth was scarlet, it had small glinting eyes.

Kingshaw got up and flapped his arms. For a moment, the bird retreated a little way off, and higher up in the sky. He began to walk rather quickly back, through the path in the corn, looking ahead of him. Stupid to be scared of a rotten bird. What could a bird do? But he felt his own extreme isolation, high up in the cornfield.

For a moment, he could only hear the soft thudding of his own footsteps, and the silky sound of the corn, brushing against him. Then, there was a rush of air, as the great crow came beating down, and wheeled about his head. The beak opened and the hoarse caaw came out again and again, from inside the scarlet mouth.

Kingshaw began to run, not caring now, if he trampled the corn, wanting to get away,

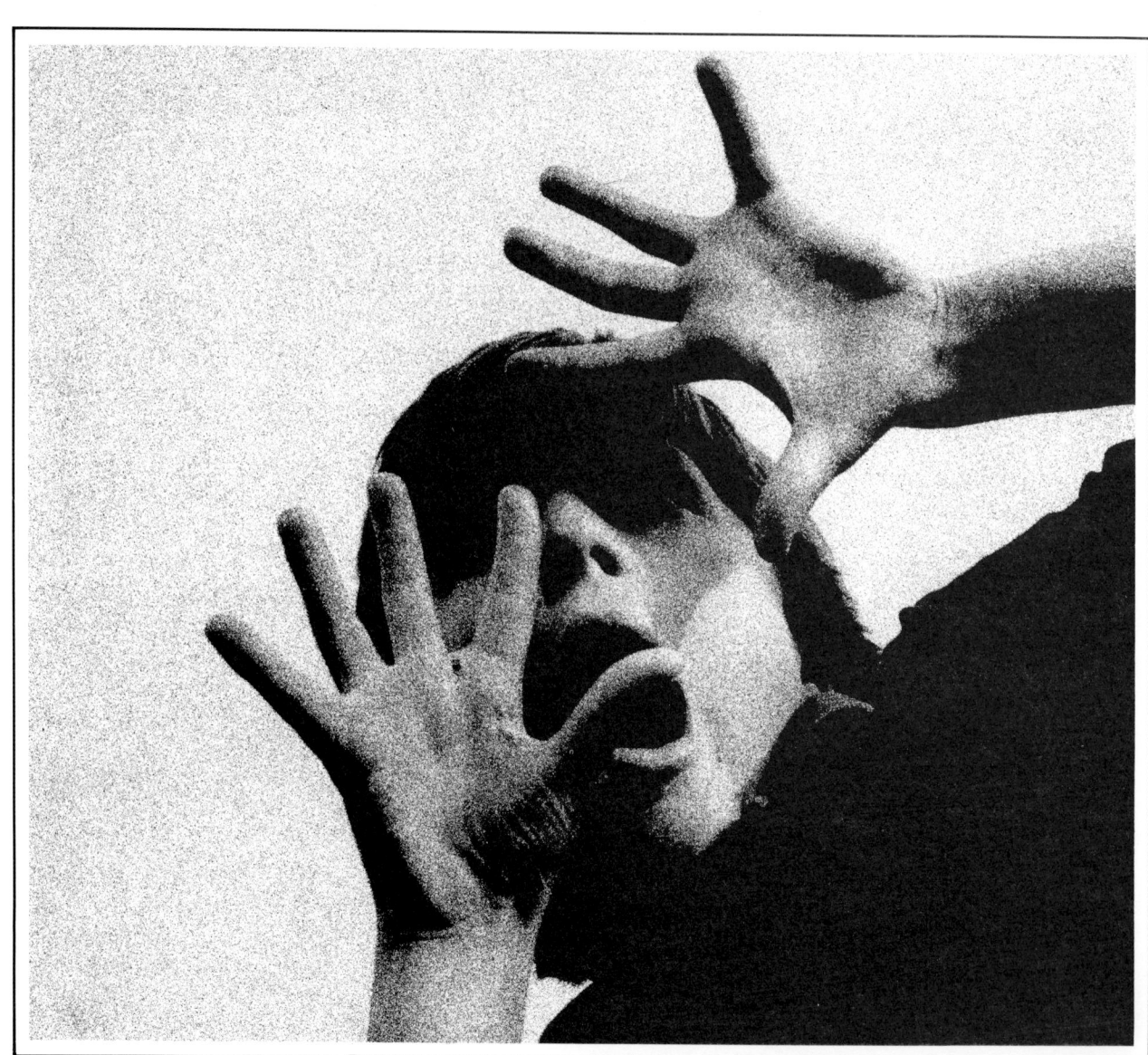

down into the next field. He thought that the corn might be some kind of crow's food store, in which he was seen as an invader. Perhaps this was only the first of a whole battalion of crows, that would rise up and swoop at him. Get on to the grass then, he thought, get on to the grass, that'll be safe, it'll go away. He wondered if it had mistaken him for some hostile animal, lurking down in the corn.

His progress was very slow, through the cornfield, the thick stalks bunched together and got in his way, and he had to shove them back with his arms. But he reached the gate and climbed it, and dropped on to the grass of the field on the other side. Sweat was running down his forehead and into his eyes. He looked up. The crow kept on coming. He ran.

But it wasn't easy to run down this field, either, because of the tractor ruts. He began to leap wildly from side to side of them, his legs stretched as wide as they could go, and for a short time, it seemed that he did go faster. The crow dived again, and, as it rose, Kingshaw felt the tip of its black wing, beating against his face. He gave a sudden, dry sob. Then, his left foot caught in one of the ruts and he keeled over, going down straight forwards.

He lay with his face in the coarse grass, panting and sobbing by turns, with the sound of his own blood pumping through his ears. He felt the sun on the back of his neck, and his ankle was wrenched. But he would be able to get up. He raised his head, and wiped two fingers across his face. A streak of blood came off, from where a thistle had scratched him. He got unsteadily to his feet, taking in deep, desperate breaths of the close air. He could not see the crow.

But when he began to walk forwards again, it rose up from the grass a little way off, and began to circle and swoop. Kingshaw broke into a run, sobbing and wiping the damp mess of tears and sweat off his face with one hand. There was a blister on his ankle, rubbed raw by the sandal strap. The crow was still quite high, soaring easily, to keep pace with him. Now, he had scrambled over the third gate, and he was in the field next to the one that belonged to Warings. He could see the back of the house. He began to run much faster.

This time, he fell and lay completely winded. Through the runnels of sweat and the sticky tufts of his own hair, he could see a figure, looking down at him from one of the top windows of the house.

Then, there was a single screech, and the terrible beating of wings, and the crow swooped down and landed in the middle of his back.

Kingshaw thought that, in the end, it must have been his screaming that frightened it off, for he dared not move. He lay and closed his eyes and felt the claws of the bird, digging into his skin, through the thin shirt, and began to scream in a queer, gasping sort of way. After a moment or two, the bird rose. He had expected it to begin pecking at him with his beak, remembering terrible stories about vultures that went for living people's eyes. He could not believe in his own escape.

He scrambled up, and ran on, and this time, the crow only hovered above, though not very high up, and still following him, but silently, and no longer attempting to swoop down. Kingshaw felt his legs go weak beneath him, as he climbed the last fence, and stood in the place from which he had started out on his walk, by the edge of the copse. He looked back fearfully. The crow circled a few times, and then dived into the thick foliage of the beech trees.

▷ What similarities are there between the two pieces? What differences? Is the intention of the two writers similar or different? Which do you find more frightening? Why? How does this incident haunt Kingshaw later in his dreams?

▷ Imagine that Kingshaw and Hooper keep diaries. Write Kingshaw's account of the attack of the crow and then Hooper's as he sees it from his bedroom window. Bring out the contrast between the two accounts. Kingshaw will be terrified, whereas Hooper will be scornful and jeering.

Creating tension – the castle

Read this piece of dialogue, which is one of the longest in the book. As you read, decide how Susan Hill uses it to create the tension so that we wonder whether one of the boys will fall off the wall.

He said, 'I'm going back now. They might have got the picnic out.'

Hooper didn't answer.

'Come on. You can do what you like, but I'm fed up with this place. There isn't anything else to see now, it's boring.'

Hooper did not move. Kingshaw looked at him closely. His face was green-white.

'Oh, hell – do you feel sick or something?'

No answer.

'Look, you'll have to go down first, because I can't get by you, it's too narrow.'

'I can't.'

'What's up? You haven't done anything to yourself, have you? Come *on*.'

'No.'

'Why not?'

'I want to get behind you.'

Kingshaw sighed. 'Thick-head, I've already told you. I'm stuck here till you move, and there isn't any other way down. You can't get behind me.'

He supposed that they must be quite high up. He hadn't thought much about it, before, because he didn't care. He never cared, however high he climbed was never high enough.

'Look, don't be a nit, Hooper, get moving.'

'I can't, I can't. I'll fall off.'

'Hell. If you didn't like it, you shouldn't have bloody well come up here, should you?'

Hooper stared at him in surprise. He was the one who swore, usually.

'*Why* did you come up?'

Hooper gave him a helpless look. His fingers were like claws, the knuckles showing white through the skin with the strain of clinging so hard on to his stone.

'You were just trying to be *clever*, weren't you?'

'It's your fault, you dared me.'

'I never did.'

'I'll fall off, I'll fall off, Kingshaw, my hands'll slip.' His voice was high and cracked with fear.

Kingshaw waited a second, thinking. Then he said, 'Now listen – you've got to do what I tell you, because I know how to get down from here and you don't, and I'm not scared and you are. You've got to do everything I tell you – right?'

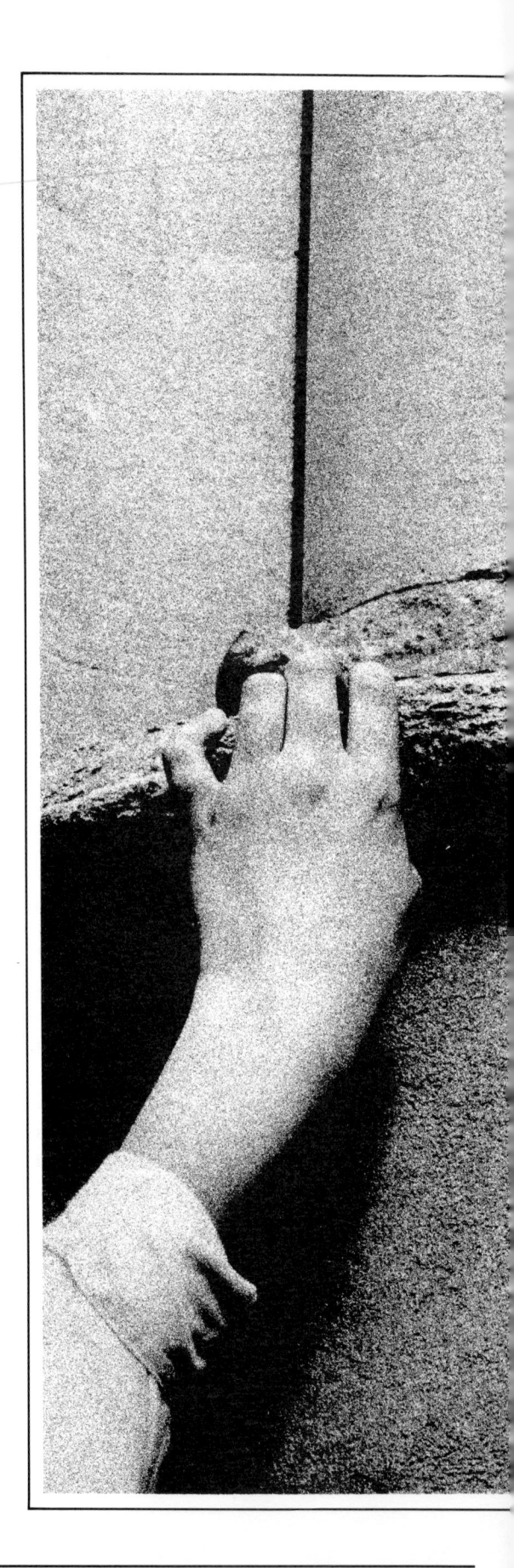

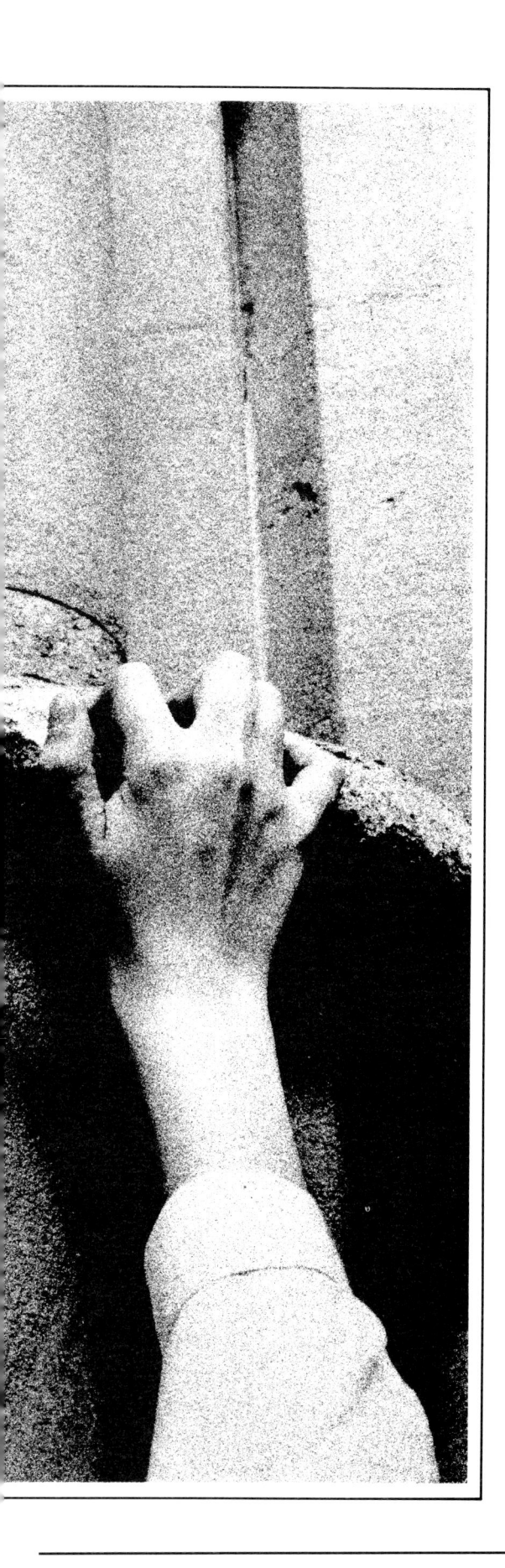

'Yes.'
'O.K. First take your hands off that wall, then.'
'No, I can't.'
'You've got to.'
'If I do, I'll just fall, I will, Kingshaw.'
'Shut up and do as you're told.'
'I *can't*. Oh, Jesus, don't make me let go. Why can't you try and get past, and then I can hold on to you?'
'Because there isn't *room* . . . How many more times?'
'If I fall off there, I'll be dead.'
'TAKE YOUR HANDS OFF THE WALL, HOOPER.'
Silence. Neither of them moved.
'HOOPER . . .' Kingshaw's voice rang round the stone walls. Slowly, Hooper began to release his hold on the stone, finger by finger.
'Promise you won't make me fall, you've got to promise.'
'You won't fall if you listen and do as I say.'
'*Promise.*'
'Oh God, you are an idiot, Hooper. O.K., I promise. Now open your eyes.'
'No.'
'*Open your eyes.*'
'I don't like it, I don't like it. I don't want to see down.'
'You haven't got to look down, you've got to look at your feet and think about what you're doing.'
Hooper opened his eyes and at once, his gaze was drawn towards the ground below. He said, 'Oh God . . .' in a whisper, and shut his eyes again, screwing them up hard, until his cheekbones rose. He had not moved his body at all.

▷ In pairs, improvise the situation in which Hooper is too terrified to move off the wall and Kingshaw is trying to help him. Bring out the contrast between Hooper's terrified high-pitched voice, and Kingshaw's calm authority.

Then practise and learn the dialogue. Decide upon the feeling behind each line and therefore how it should be said. You should find a great variety of feeling – for instance panic, irritation, resignation, taunting, authority, weakness, fear, desperation, exasperation.

▷ Choose another piece of dialogue in which tension is created and prepare and practise it in the same way.

Kingshaw's suicide

He knew, quite suddenly, what to do.

▷ In groups, discuss all the factors which led Kingshaw to commit suicide and to commit it in that particular place.

Susan Hill writes:

> 'I have often been taken to task for the ending of the novel. It couldn't, wouldn't happen, it is melodramatic and unlikely, it *shouldn't* happen. No boy of eleven would commit suicide because he's afraid of a bully.
>
> But boys of eleven *have* committed suicide for what, to the adult outsider, might seem even flimsier reasons. . . . I believed in his suicide when I made it happen, and re-reading the book, I believe in it all over again.'

▷ Do you believe in Kingshaw's suicide, or do you share the view of those who say it couldn't happen? Discuss your reasons.

▷ In groups of four, each take one of these roles – Mr Hooper, Mrs Kingshaw, Edmund, a reporter. The reporter questions each character in turn soon after the body has been found. Find out what each knows and thinks about what has happened.

▷ Use what you have learnt from the previous assignment to write a newspaper report for one of the popular daily newspapers. Use these guidelines to help you.

1. Invent a headline which seizes the reader's attention.
2. Arouse curiosity as to why Kingshaw killed himself and suggest reasons.
3. Present the *facts* – names, ages, addresses – about the people involved.
4. Include quotations from Mr Hooper, Mrs Kingshaw and Edmund.

Susan Hill

The future

'I cannot hold out much hope for the remaining trio achieving a contented family life, for Hooper becoming a mature, well-integrated, happy adult human being, given their respective personalities, and with the shadow of Kingshaw's suicide hanging over them all, forever.'

Susan Hill

The shadow hanging over them

▷ Imagine that it is a year after Kingshaw's suicide, and the Hoopers are going on a picnic to a nearby beauty spot with a park and a lake. Write an account of the day, after considering these suggestions:

1 How do these final lines from the novel indicate Hooper's and Mrs Kingshaw's reactions to the situation and how do they point forward to their relationship in the future?

When he saw Kingshaw's body, upside down in the water, Hooper thought suddenly, it was because of me, I did that, *it was because of me*, and a spurt of triumph went through him.

'Now it's all right, Edmund dear, everything is all right.' Mrs Helena Kingshaw put an arm out towards him, held him to her. 'I don't want you to look, dear, you mustn't look and be upset, everything is all right.'

Hooper felt the damp cloth of her coat, pressed against his face, and smelled her perfumey smell. Then, there was the sound of the men, splashing through the water.

2 Are the parents more protective towards Edmund?

3 Do they overcompensate out of guilt after the incident at the castle and after Kingshaw's suicide?

4 How does Mrs Hooper feel towards her new son?

5 Does Edmund use Kingshaw's death as a means of getting his own way or of upsetting the grown-ups?

6 How will you create and use the setting in the way that, for instance, Susan Hill uses Hang Wood or Leydell Castle? Will Edmund boat on or swim in the lake?

7 Will Edmund meet and befriend a boy who is also on a day out? What will the boy be like? How will he treat him?

8 How will Mr and Mrs Hooper get on after a year of marriage? Has Kingshaw's death affected their marriage? Do they ever talk about him? If so, how?

Parallel themes in other works by Susan Hill

'Almost all imaginative writers have obsessions – subjects, themes, images, character-types, settings – which recur over and over again in their work.

One of my strongest and regularly recurring obsessions has been with childhood; my own, indirectly, but more, the state of childhood; what it feels like, how it truly is and how adults interpret it. And particularly, I have been interested in children who are in some way at odds with the rest of the world.'

Susan Hill

In her short stories you will find many of the themes that interest Susan Hill in *I'm the King of the Castle*.

Study these extracts from her short stories and find parallel passages from *I'm the King of the Castle*.

'The Albatross'

Duncan, Dafty Duncan, as he is known in the village, is a simple boy who is over protected by his invalid mother. He wants to be accepted by the men in the fishing village, particularly Ted Flint, his hero. In the first passage we see him invited by Ted to go fishing out to sea and being torn by anxiety as to whether he should go.

▷ In what ways is he similar to Kingshaw in the book? In what ways different?

What character in *I'm the King of the Castle* is like or has a similar function to Ted Flint?

The boat was down and ready, the motor running. Ted Flint was standing up in it, towering above Duncan, tall as a king.
 'Get in then, if you're coming.'
 Why should he take me out there, Duncan thought. *Why*? I've never been, I don't know anything, he doesn't speak to me, why should he ask me to go? Though he could sense no animosity in Ted Flint, no threat of danger. He was entirely puzzled.
 A wave gathered, battleship-grey and seething along its crest, and then crashed over. The boat lifted and rocked.
 'Hey?'
 There was a moment when Duncan was ready to spring forwards and up, when he

could already feel himself going out to sea, imagine the movement of it beneath him, they were pushing ahead. 'Want to come out in the boat then?' With Ted Flint. *I could go.*

And then another wave began to gather, and suddenly, he saw them coming at him, one after the next, rising up higher and higher, ready to break about his head and drag him down into them, and he knew that once they had pushed the boat out, then there would be no escape for him, he would be alone with Ted Flint, towering above him, in the middle of the endless sky and heaving sea, and he was seized with choking panic, he turned and began to run, pounding off down the beach to get away from the menace of the waves and wind, and the chugging of the boat, out of the reach of Ted Flint, he would have done anything rather than go on that sea.

'That's not safe, you'd never manage, you'd not know what to do. You leave going in boats alone.'

He reached the steps and scrambled up and raced over the square, making for the dark, close safety of Wash Alley. Later, he would think of the folly of it, and want to claw at himself in helpless anger, later, he would ask again and again what Ted Flint had thought and said, knowing that there would never in his life be a second chance. He had not dared to go out in a boat, he had been overcome with terror at the sight of the sea, he had run away. So what they said about him was true.

In the second extract, Duncan explores the house of the lady in whose garden he works, while she is absent.

▷ What impression do you get of the room? What impression do you get of Duncan's feelings?

What characteristic of Susan Hill's writing does this passage illustrate?

There was nobody else in the house. When he closed the door of the kitchen and stood in the wide hall, everything seemed to settle around him, it was entirely still. The sun came through a round pane of glass in the front door. He began to go about the place, very quietly, into every room, feeling the different feel under his shoes, smelling the strange smells. There was pale waxed wood and the thick knotted pile of rugs, the colours of the drawing-room were gold and white and lemon in the sun. He had touched things gently, feeling the texture of silk cushions, roughened against his skin, lifting up a paper knife from the desk beside the window and balancing it. Upstairs, the bedroom overlooked the empty garden. It had wide windows and corn-coloured curtains, and smelled of Mrs Reddingham-Lee, as though her scented powder hung about on the air. He was inquisitive about everything here, wanting to touch each chair and picture and ornament, to open cupboards and drawers and stare inside. But he had moved about cautiously, his nerves alert just below the skin, hearing the seething of the dust. He thought, this is what they have, this and this and this, here is where they eat, and laugh and sit and sleep, this is all of theirs. He had never seen what it was like before. The rooms were all long and high and bright with the afternoon sun, but he felt as though, if he breathed out too quickly, the things about him might splinter and break. He touched his fingers slowly down on to the white piano keys and they were cool, the notes sounded faintly, vibrating far away down the strings. He wanted to stay here. Outside, he saw the shimmer of heat over the garden.

After a long time, he had gone and the rooms had settled back into themselves again, when he looked behind him anxiously, he could see no trace of his own presence there.

When he was fumbling to tie back some raspberry canes, Mrs Reddingham-Lee returned. Watching her put her legs out of the blue car, and stand up, he thought, I know everything about you, I know secrets. Though later he had realized that it was nothing, that he knew only curtains and tables and vases and chairs, the smell of a bedroom. Nothing.

In the following extract from 'The Elephant Man', William is a sensitive boy who has been taken to a children's party in an expensive hotel, where he knows nobody. He does not enjoy parties anyway because he too is an outsider.

▷ In what ways is he similar to Kingshaw? In what ways different? What fears of Kingshaw's does he share?

▷ What situation in I'm the King of the Castle is it similar to?
How does Susan Hill create a sense of nightmare?

'The Elephant Man'

William stood, thinking of Nanny Fawcett and the friend, far away down all the carpeted stairs, eating tea in the empty lounge.

As it went on, it became like all the other parties he had known, the terrors were at least familiar, the awful taste of the tea and of trifles in little, waxed paper cases and the staring of the bigger girls. There were games which he did not win and dancing for which he had not brought his pumps. The woman in mauve clapped her hands and laughed a lot and changed the records on the gramophone, and from time to time, she took his hand and led him closer into the circle of the others. 'You are to look after this little boy, you are to be kind to William now, dear, try and remember.'

But then, suddenly one of the hotel waiters had drawn the curtains and they were all made to sit tightly together on the carpeted floor, squealing a little with apprehension and excitement. Then the music began. Oh God, Oh God, make it not be a conjuror or a Punch and Judy, William thought, pressing his nails deeply into the palms of his hands. But it was not, it was something he had never seen before, something worse.

The area ahead of them was lit like a stage, with a high stool placed there, and then a figure came lumbering out of the darkness. From the shoulders down it was a man, his costume all in one piece and wumbling as it moved, like the covering on a pantomime horse. But it stood upon only two legs and the legs were three times, ten times, as long as human legs, and oddly stiff at the joints. Above the shoulders, the huge head was not a man's head, but that of an elephant, nodding and bobbing and bending forward to the music and waving its disgusting trunk.

William sat and every so often closed his eyes, willing for it to be gone, for the curtains to be drawn again and the ordinary January daylight to flood the room. But he could still hear the music and when that stopped, the elephant man spoke and sang, the voice very deep, distorted and hollow, booming away inside the huge head. He opened his eyes and did not want to look, but he could not stop himself, the square of light and then the lurching animal man drew him. It was dancing, lifting its huge legs up and down stiffly, clapping its hands together, while the head nodded. From somewhere, it produced a vividly coloured stuffed parrot, which sat upon its shoulder and answered back to jokes, in a terrible rasping voice. Then the music started again.

'Now, children, now what about everybody doing a little dance with me, what about us all dancing together? Would you like that?'

'Yes,' they yelled. 'Yes, Yes!' and clapped and bounced up and down.

'And what about somebody coming up on my shoulder and being as high as the sky, what about that? Would you like to do that?

'Yes,' they screamed. 'Yes, yes!' and rushed forwards, clamouring about the baggy legs, clutching and laughing.

From the gramophone came the music for a Conga, and the elephant man set off with everyone clinging on behind in a chain, prancing about the room, and first one, then another was lifted high up on to its great shoulders, swaying with delight, hands touching the ceiling, swinging the chandelier. William stood back against the wall in the darkness, praying not to be noticed, but when the line reached him, he was noticed, the woman in mauve clucked and took his hand, putting him in with the others, so that he was forced to trot on one leg and then the next to the music. And then, suddenly, he felt the elephant man behind him, and he was lifted up, the hands digging tightly into his sides, and he could neither scream nor protest, he could scarcely breathe, only dangle helplessly there, near to the cream-painted ceiling, and see, far below him, the upturned, mocking faces of the others, hear the blast of the music. Through the slits in the elephant head, he could see eyes, flickering like

lanterns in a turnip, and he looked away dizzy, praying to be set down.
   At the end, the lights did not go on immediately, he could slip out of the door and nobody noticed him.

'Friends of Miss Reece'

The boy in this story (who is not given a name) is often left to spend the night at his aunt's nursing home for the elderly – hardly the place for a young boy – while his parents are out enjoying themselves at parties and dinners.

▷ What similarities are there in the way the mother speaks and the way Mrs Kingshaw speaks in *I'm the King of the Castle*?

What is similar about the way the mothers treat their sons? What do the sons have in common?

'We are going out until very late. It will be much nicer for you to sleep at the nursing home,' his mother had said. 'It will be a treat.'
   He had looked away and out of the window, on to the garden, where the last of the melting snow lay, grubby as the stained linen that came down to Aunt Spencer's washroom in a hand-operated lift.
   He would have said, I don't want to, I want to stay here, I don't like sleeping there all night, because of Wetherby. Once, he had half-spoken.
   '*Nurse* Wetherby, to you, and you are very silly about her.'
   'She's ugly.'
   'Not everybody can be beautiful.'
   'Her teeth are all yellow.'
   'That is a nasty, *personal* remark, polite little boys do not say things like that.'
   'She. . .'
   But he could not have told. He kept his mind turned from the thought of the upstairs landings of the Cedars Lawn Nursing Home, and the attic where he must sleep, in the room next to Wetherby.
   'Are you going to a ball?'
   'No, dear,'
   'To a dinner?'
   For they were always putting on new clothes and getting into the warm car and driving off somewhere. The names of the people whose houses they visited were familiar as those of the streets and squares around which he walked, every afternoon, with the girl Shirley, who was paid to take him out, by the hour.

Longman Imprint Books

I'm the King of the Castle *Susan Hill*

ISBN 0 582 22173 0

This edition of the novel has an introduction specially written by Susan Hill. In addition, notes and points for discussion are included together with an extract from *The Albatross* and an extract from *A Change for the Better*.

A selection of novels and stories from Longman Imprint Books, Longman Study Texts and Modern Women Writers:

Longman Study Texts

July's People by Nadine Gordimer
The Cone-Gatherers by Robin Jenkins
Paradise Postponed by John Mortimer
Animal Farm by George Orwell
Nineteen Eighty-Four by George Orwell
Staying On by Paul Scott
The History of Mr Polly by H G Wells

Modern Women Writers

Hotel du Lac by Anita Brookner
My Brilliant Career by Miles Franklin
City of Illusions by Ursula Le Guin
Edith Jackson by Rosa Guy
The Albatross and other stories by Susan Hill
Heat and Dust by Ruth Prawer Jhabvala

Longman Imprint Books

I'm the King of the Castle by Susan Hill
Strange Meeting by Susan Hill

Titles in the Longman Literature Guidelines series:

Animal Farm
The Diary of Anne Frank
An Inspector Calls
The Winslow Boy
Romeo and Juliet
Macbeth
I'm the King of the Castle

Acknowledgements

We are grateful to the following for permission to reproduce copyright material:

The Bodley Head for an extract from *The Dark is Rising* by Susan Cooper; Jonathan Cape Ltd for poem 'First Day At School' by Roger McGough from *In the Glassroom*; Faber & Faber Ltd for poem 'The Dare' by Judith Nicholls from *Midnight Forest and Other Poems*; Hamish Hamilton Ltd for an extract from *I'm the King of the Castle* by Susan Hill; Authors' Agents for an extract from pp 18–19 *A Kestral for a Knave* by Barry Hines. (c) Barry Hines 1967; Authors' Agents for extracts from the short stories 'The Albatross', 'The Elephant Man', 'The Friends of Miss Reece' by Susan Hill from *The Albatross and Other Stories* pubd. Hamish Hamilton Ltd; Macmillan London & Basingstoke for an extract from *The Machine Gunners* by Robert Westall.

We are grateful to the following for permission to reproduce photographs:

Martin Adams, page 14; J. Allan Cash, page 33; Donald Cooper c Photostage, page 13; James Drennan, page 46; GSF Picture Library, page 43, Ronald Grant, pages 25, 26; Camilla Jessel, pages 22–23; Franta Provaznik, page 40; Catherine Shakespeare Lane, pages 2, 4, 5, 8, 10, 21, 28, 36, 38–39; Tony Stone Worldwide, page 6 (photo: Beryl Bidwell); c Photograph by Janine Wiedel, page 32.

Cover photograph by Catherine Shakespeare Lane.

Series designed by Jenny Palmer of Pentaprism

LONGMAN GROUP UK LIMITED,
Longman House, Burnt Mill, Harlow,
Essex CM20 2JE, England,
and Associated Companies throughout the world.
© Longman Group UK Limited 1989
All rights reserved, no part of this publication may be reproduced, stored in a retrieval system, or transmitted in any form or by any means, electronic, mechanical, photocopying, recording, or otherwise, without either the prior written permission of the Publishers or a licence permitting restricted copying issued by the Copyright Licensing Agency Ltd, 33–34 Alfred Place, London WC1E 7DP.

First published 1989

Set in 10.5/12.5PT Cheltenham Light and 10.5/13PT Helvetica. LINOTRON 202

*Produced by Longman Group (F.E.) Ltd.
Printed in Hong Kong.*

ISBN 0 582 02174 X